MW00885462

THIS BOOK BELONGS TO:

_____

_____

_____

Copyright © 2023. By Frolic Fox. All Right Reserved

TEST COLOR PAGE

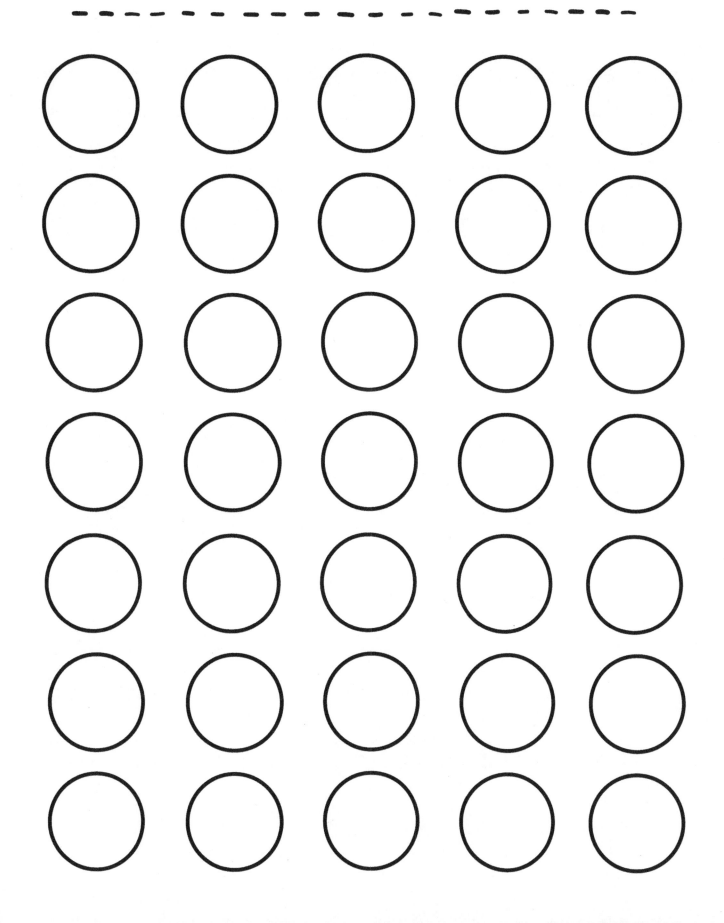

DID YOU KNOW?

Elephants have long **trunks**, which they use to breathe, smell, drink, and even pick things up. They love eating **grass**, **fruits**, and **tree bark**.

DID YOU KNOW?

Parrots are colorful and chatty birds. They can **mimic sounds** and even repeat words they hear. **Fruits, nuts,** and **seeds** are their favorite snacks.

DID YOU KNOW?

Giraffes are the tallest animals on land. Their **long necks** help them reach leaves high up in trees.

DID YOU KNOW?
Every **zebra** has a unique pattern of stripes. No two **zebras** look exactly alike. In the wild, **zebras** mostly eat grass, but they also munch on shrubs, herbs, and twigs.

DID YOU KNOW?

Koalas live in trees and love eating **eucalyptus leaves**. They eat a little and sleep up to 20 hours a day because leaves give them little energy.

DID YOU KNOW?

Turtles are known for their **sturdy shells**, which protect them. They can live in water or on land, eating **plants, insects,** and **small fish.** Some turtles can live for a very long time!

DID YOU KNOW?

Butterflies start as caterpillars and then transform into beautiful flying wonders. They flutter around, sipping nectar from flowers with their long tongues.

DID YOU KNOW?

Manatees, also called **sea cows**, glide gracefully underwater. They're **herbivores**, enjoying a diet of **seagrass** and **freshwater plants**. Their gentle nature makes them loved by many.

DID YOU KNOW?

Toucans are known for their big, **colorful beaks**. They live in treetops and enjoy feasting on fruits, making the rainforest lively with their calls.

DID YOU KNOW?

Deer are graceful with big antlers. They love to eat grass, berries, and leaves. If you see one, you might notice it can run and jump really quickly!

DID YOU KNOW?

Fluffy **sheep** give us cozy wool. They spend their days grazing on green grass and like to stay close to their herd friends.

DID YOU KNOW?

Peacocks are known for their amazing **tail feathers**. When they fan them out, it's a colorful show! They like to eat seeds, fruits, and small insects.

DID YOU KNOW?
Rhinos are big and strong with tough skin. Their large horn helps them defend the territory. Sometimes, they like to splash in the mud to cool off.

DID YOU KNOW?

Elegant and white, **swans** glide on water with *grace*. They stretch their long necks to find underwater plants to eat and are often seen in pairs, showing loyalty.

DID YOU KNOW?

Frogs are great jumpers with a love for water. They have a smooth, moist skin and enjoy catching bugs with their long, sticky tongues.

DID YOU KNOW?

Squirrels are quick and curious. With bushy tails and sharp claws, they climb trees to find nuts and seeds, storing them for later.

DID YOU KNOW?

Bats flap through the night, using special sounds to find their way. They love eating insects or fruits, and during the day, they hang **upside-down** to rest.

DID YOU KNOW?

With masked faces and bushy tails, **raccoons** are curious and clever. They use their hands to explore and find food, like fruits, nuts, and even fish from streams.

DID YOU KNOW?

Dolphins are smart and friendly sea creatures. They love to jump and play in waves and communicate with clicks and whistles.

Made in the USA
Las Vegas, NV
30 November 2024

12986438R00059